Policy and Procedures Manual for Heartfelt Care Services Limited

Heartfelt Care Services Limited
Team

ISBN: 9798339301813

Dedication

This work is dedicated to the countless healthcare and retail professionals whose dedication and compassion form the backbone of our communities. To the caregivers, support workers, and employees who go above and beyond daily; your commitment inspires us to strive for excellence in everything we do.

Heartfelt Care Services Limited is also dedicated to the clients and organizations who trust us to meet their staffing needs. Your partnership drives our mission to create meaningful connections between talented individuals and the businesses that need them most.

Finally, to the visionaries and team members who believe in the power of making a difference, this is for you. Your unwavering passion and hard work lay the foundation for a brighter, more connected future in workforce management. Thank you for being part of this journey.

ACKNOWLEDGMENTS

Heartfelt Care Services Limited sincerely wishes to thank everyone who has helped us on our journey.
To our clients, thank you for trusting our agency and allowing us to support your staffing needs.
To our dedicated candidates and staff members, your hard work and unwavering commitment to excellence make all the difference. Your passion and professionalism bring our vision to life every single day.
Lastly, we express profound appreciation to our family, friends, and supporters who have encouraged and motivated us every step of the way. Your belief in our mission makes us confident, fueling our determination to grow and succeed.
Thank you all for being a part of the Heartfelt Care Services Limited story

Policy and Procedures Manual for Heartfelt Care
Services Limited

Introduction

Purpose:

This manual provides guidelines and procedures to ensure the consistent operation of Heartfelt Care Services Limited, compliance with relevant regulations, and high service delivery standards.

Scope:

This manual applies to all Heartfelt Care Services Limited employees, consultants, and contractors.

Company Policies

2.1 Equal Opportunity Employment Policy
Statement:

Heartfelt Care Services Limited: A Champion of Equal Employment Opportunities Policy
Statement:

Procedures:

All job postings must include an equal opportunity statement.

Recruitment, hiring, training, promotion, and termination decisions must be based on merit and business needs. Non-compliance may result in disciplinary action.

Report any discrimination or harassment incidents to the HR department, which will handle the investigation and resolution process.

2.2 Code of Conduct Policy Statement:

The employees must focus on the highest ethical conduct standards in all business activities.

Procedures:

Maintain professionalism and integrity in all interactions.

Refrain from engaging in activities that could conflict with personal interests and professional duties and inform management if such conflicts arise.

Protect confidential information and intellectual property.

2.3 Data Protection and Privacy Policy Statement:

Heartfelt Care Services Limited is committed to protecting the privacy and confidentiality of personal data.

Procedures:

Adhere to GDPR and all applicable Follow data protection Regulations to protect confidentiality and ensure the integrity of personal data.

Obtain consent from candidates and clients before collecting personal data.

Establish protective measures to prevent unauthorized access and potential data breaches.

Provide data protection training to employees. 2.4 Health and Safety Policy Statement:

Heartfelt Care Services Limited prioritizes its employees' and clients' health and safety.

Procedures:

Perform routine risk assessments and safety inspections to detect potential hazards and ensure a safe working environment for all employees.

Provide health and safety training to employees. Ensure compliance with health and safety regulations. Report and investigate any workplace accidents or incidents.

HEARTFELT CARE SERVICES' LIMITED
COMMUNICATION POLICY
Communication Policy and Procedures

Purpose: To provide information and guidance to staff about **Heartfelt Care Services Limited's** expectations when communicating. It will include service users, friends, family, staff, multidisciplinary team members and others.

There are many reasons a person may not be able to communicate. Staff must recognise these so that they can pay particular attention to how they communicate with these people.

Reasons might include:

- Sensory impairment, e.g. visual problems, hearing difficulties or speech impediments.

- Health problems, e.g. dementia, strokes or terminal illnesses such as brain tumours or tumours on the vocal cords. Neurological conditions such as motor neurone or Huntingdon's disease. Genetic problems such as Down's syndrome or a learning disability. Infections or pain.

- Mental incapacity. It might include being under the influence of alcohol, drugs or medication. The presence of a brain tumour, dementia or a stroke.

- Environmental issues, e.g. noise, poor lighting or distractions.

- Psychological problems such as anger, denial, fear, anxiety and bereavement.

This policy includes the requirements of the Accessible Information Standard (AIS) 2017, which relates to the information and communication needs of people with disabilities, impairments, or sensory loss.

Definitions: Heartfelt Care Services Limited commits to equality in communication and expects that all communication is effective.

For clarification, **Heartfelt Care Services Limited** uses the AIS definitions for disability, impairment or sensory loss.

Disability—NHS England uses the definition in the Equality Act 2010 to define disability as a *physical or mental impairment* that has a *'long-term adverse effect on the person's ability to carry out normal day-to-day activities.'*

Impairment – The authors use the Scope definition for this, i.e. the *'long-term limitation of a person's physical, mental or sensory function.'*

Sensory loss—This is mainly for people who are blind or have some vision loss, deaf/deaf, have some hearing loss, or are deafblind.

Policy: Heartfelt Care Services Limited is committed to equality. It expects that all communication is effective, in line with the AIS, and anti-discriminatory, as required by the Equality Act (2010).

Managers and staff must ensure that people with disabilities, impairments, or sensory loss understand what is being said when communicating. They should do this by requesting feedback to check understanding.

When communicating with others, **Heartfelt Care Services Limited** expects staff to:

- Find the best method of communicating with the person. Help the person use this method to promote two-way communication and understanding.

- Professionally speak to others by always treating people with courtesy, respect and consideration.

- Communicate directly with the person or persons to resolve any differences that might develop. Staff should handle differences of opinion privately and with tact.

Heartfelt Care Services Limited will not tolerate gossip and backbiting.

- Maintain a respectful working atmosphere.

- Refrain from shouting, yelling, using vulgarities or swearing at staff, service users or others.

- Avoid discriminatory remarks relating to any of the nine protected characteristics of the Equality Act 2010. These include appearance, dress, and other non-work-related matters, such as where people live, socialise, etc.

Heartfelt Care Services Limited will regard breaches of this policy as misconduct.

Scope: This policy contains information and guidance developed from:

- Regulations 10 (Dignity and Respect) and 11 (Consent) of the Health and Social Care Act 2008 (Regulated Activities) Regulations 2014.

- The Equality Act (2010).

- Accessible Information Standard 2017.

Heartfelt Care Services Limited expect staff to adhere to this legislation through the implementation of the policy.

The registered manager should regularly check guidance from relevant bodies to ensure this policy is up to date.

This policy applies to all staff working for **Heartfelt Care Services Limited.**

Procedures

Assessment and care planning

- The AIS requires staff to identify the communication and information needs of people with disabilities, impairments, or sensory loss.

- Staff will identify communication and information needs during the initial assessment and continue to do so regularly to always ensure effective communication.

- Managers will develop care plans that flag service users' communication and information needs. They should share these with other staff, so they know how to communicate with the person.

Helping effective communication

- As part of the AIS, service users must receive information in an accessible format. It might include using various aids or tools to help with understanding. For example, the material is written in Braille. Material translated into another language. An interpreter will explain a treatment or communication via high-tech equipment.

- Before communication takes place, staff should ensure the person is in the right frame of mind. Staff should postpone communication if the person is angry or distracted or if the environment is unsuitable.

- Staff should be aware of invading a service user's personal space, as this can prevent effective communication.

- When communicating verbally, staff should ensure that their language, tone, pace, volume, and pitch are clear. Their body language should match the message they are conveying.

- Staff should summarise what they have said and ask for confirmation that the person understands this.

- Active listening skills are difficult for people to grasp. However, staff must try to hear the service user's words without interruption. They must only act on the information when the person has finished their point.

- Avoid making judgements about others. For example, do not compare, criticise or blame others, as this can prevent the person from talking to staff.

Communication aids and equipment

- If the service user needs assistance or communication equipment, staff should discuss this with the person. They may need an assessment to ensure the equipment suits that individual. A local speech and language therapist or TEC personnel can help with this.

- There may be times when you need to translate literature or language for the person. It might involve an interpreting or translation service, such as Language Line. Make sure the organisation understands the importance of confidentiality.

Recruitment and Placement Procedures

3.1 Recruitment Process Policy
Statement:
Heartfelt Care Services Limited is dedicated to recruiting the best candidates fairly and transparently, ensuring everyone is given equal opportunities.
Procedures:

Job Posting: Advertise job openings on relevant platforms.

Application: Collect and screen applications.

Interview: Conduct interviews with shortlisted candidates.

Selection: Select the best candidate based on qualifications and fit.

Onboarding: Provide new hires with an orientation and training program. 3.2 Candidate Screening Policy Statement:

At Heartfelt Care Services Limited, we leave no stone unturned to ensure that all candidates meet our high standards and provide our employees with a secure and trustworthy environment.

Procedures:

Verify candidate qualifications and experience. Conduct background checks, including criminal record checks.

Check professional references.

Ensure candidates have the necessary certifications and licenses. 3.3 Client Engagement Policy Statement:

Heartfelt Care Services Limited is dedicated to Building Solid Client Relationships Policy Statement:

Procedures:

Initial Consultation: Understand client needs and requirements.

Service Agreement: Draft and sign a service agreement outlining terms and conditions.

Placement: Match suitable candidates with client requirements.

Follow-Up: Maintain regular contact with clients to ensure satisfaction.

Employment Services Procedures

4.1 Employee Management Policy
Statement:

Heartfelt Care Services Limited manages its employees to ensure high-quality service delivery.

Procedures:

Payroll: Process employee salaries and benefits accurately and timely.

Training: Provide ongoing training and development opportunities.

Performance Review: Conduct regular performance evaluations.

Compliance: Ensure employees comply with company policies and regulations. 4.2 Service Provision Policy Statement:

Heartfelt Care Services Limited is committed to delivering high-quality care services.

Procedures:

Care Plan: Develop a detailed care plan for each Client.

Staff Deployment: Assign qualified staff to client locations.

Quality Assurance: Conduct regular quality checks and client feedback surveys.

Incident Reporting: Document and address any incidents or complaints promptly.

Compliance and Regulatory Procedures

5.1 Regulatory Compliance Policy
Statement:

Heartfelt Care Services Limited complies with all relevant laws and regulations.

Procedures:

Stay updated with changes in employment and healthcare regulations.

Conduct regular compliance audits.

Provide compliance training to employees.

Maintain accurate records and documentation. 5.2 Complaints and Grievances Policy Statement:

Heartfelt Care Services Limited addresses all complaints and grievances fairly and promptly.

Procedures:

Complaint Submission: Clients and employees can submit complaints via email or a complaint form.

Investigation: Investigate the complaint thoroughly.

Resolution: Provide a resolution within a specified timeframe.

Follow-Up: Ensure the resolution is satisfactory to all parties involved.

HEARTFELT CARE SERVICES LIMITED COMPLAINTS POLICY AND PROCEDURE
Complaints Policy

Purpose: To outline the information and guidance for staff to follow on managing comments and complaints to the service.

Policy: Heartfelt Care Services Limited is committed to providing a high-quality service. When something goes wrong with our care, treatment or service provision, you need to know about this to improve the care you provide. To achieve this, Heartfelt Care Services Limited will:

- Encourage comments, suggestions, observations and complaints and act upon these as a continual improvement.

- Make sure staff accept comments or complaints professionally and without recrimination.

- Make the system easy to use.

- Thank people formally for any compliments, comments, suggestions and observations.

- Make sure you respond to and investigate complaints fairly and within the time frame.

- Put anything that has gone wrong right and repair any damaged relationships.

Scope: The legislation and guidance staff must adhere to include:

- Care Quality Commission - Health and Social Care Act 2008 (Regulated Activities) Regulations 2014.

- Guidance for providers on meeting the regulations: Health and Social Care Act 2008 (Regulated Activities) Regulations 2014 (Part 3) (as amended): Care Quality Commission (Registration) Regulations 2009 (Part 4) (as amended).

- <Add in others relevant to the organisation>.

Definitions

Comment or observation – a verbal or written remark expressing an opinion about an aspect of the care or treatment your staff provide or about your service. An example of this might be, 'Your staff looked rushed off their feet today.'

Suggestion – a verbal or written idea about how you can change, improve or update the care or treatment your staff provide or about your service. An example might be, 'Can you send your newsletter around more regularly?'

Compliment – part of your complaint's procedure is to look at what you are doing well. Letters, cards, or verbal expressions of appreciation you receive are evidence that you are doing a good job, so you should continue to do what you are already doing well. An example might be, 'Your staff are accommodating.'

Complaint – any expression of dissatisfaction with the care or treatment your staff provide or a failure of your organisation to provide a service to a service user. This can be either written or verbal. It doesn't matter whether your staff feel this is justified or not. An example might be, 'My father has fallen every day this week.'

<Add in a time limit if you want to limit the time for when complaints should be received, e.g. within 12 months of the event occurring>

<Add in how you will investigate and respond to anonymous comments or complaints, e.g., this could be to place these onto your website via a 'service improvement' page>

Procedures

1. Receiving Comments, Observations, Suggestions and Complaints

All staff should know the definitions of a comment, observation, suggestion and complaint.

All staff should be able to take details of comments, observations, and suggestions in person and thank the person for taking the time to give these. They should pass these on to the complaint's coordinator, who will respond formally and thank the responsible person.

All staff should be able to take details of a complaint in person or give the complainant details of the complaint's coordinator or an independent advocate who can take the complaint on the complainant's behalf. <Add in who you will /will not accept complaints from if applicable>.

Staff should be able to explain that the complaint can be made verbally or in writing and that this can be done by letter to <insert address>, email to < insert email address>, telephone to <insert telephone number> or face to face <insert the name and contact details of who will do this>.

Staff should give details of the time frames for acknowledgement <insert time frame, i.e. 48 hours>. You will send a formal letter of acknowledgement to the person giving details of the next steps.

Start a complaints report containing the dates of responses, details of any investigations, the outcomes, and the dates of final letters and responses.

2. Investigating the Complaint

An investigation of the complaint will take place in the first instance by the <complaints coordinator or another person> unless the complaint is about them, and then you will ask <insert the name of the person who will investigate on your behalf in this instance>.

An investigation may involve:

•	Carrying out a record review, reviewing accident books, incident reports etc.

•	Reviewing any correspondence about the matter.

- Interviewing the staff member involved or other staff (or the complainant if further information is required).

- Observing practice.

- Reviewing policies and procedures to find discrepancies between policy and practice.

- Looking for other evidence, e.g. CCTV footage.

3. Responses

The complaints coordinator will write to the complainant on behalf of Heartfelt Care Services Limited with the outcome of the complaint.

Investigation, resolution and the final response will occur within <insert time frame, i.e. 4 weeks> as far as possible. If this is to take longer, you will inform the complainant as soon as possible.

The final response will include the details of the investigation, the outcome, and what you will do to change the practice accordingly (if appropriate).

The final response will detail how the person can escalate their complaint if unsatisfied with the outcome.

4. Improvements

The complaints coordinator will inform the registered manager of any improvements that need to be made because of the complaint so that you can develop an action plan to improve practice accordingly.

Heartfelt Care Services Limited will implement any changes to practice within <insert timeframe, e.g. 4 weeks> of the action being identified.

5. Recording

Once Heartfelt Care Services Limited has received a complaint, the complaint will be recorded. This is to include:

- The date of receipt of the complaint.

- The date of the acknowledgement of its receipt.

- You keep a copy of the acknowledgement on file.

- The date by which you will complete the investigation.

- Details of the investigation.

- Details of the outcome of the investigation.

- The date by which you will send the final letter of response.

- You will keep a copy of the final response letter on file.

- Action plans to improve practice.

6. Review

A review of the comment and complaints policy and system takes place each year or when the following occurs:

- A comment or complaint suggests the system is not working as it should.

Training and Development

Policy Statement:

Heartfelt Care Services Limited invests in the continuous development of its employees.

Procedures:

Training Needs Assessment: Identify training needs based on job requirements and performance reviews.

Training Programs: Offer relevant training programs, workshops, and seminars.

Evaluation: Assess the effectiveness of training programs through feedback and performance improvement.

Health and Safety Procedures

7.1 Workplace Safety Policy
Statement:

Heartfelt Care Services Limited ensures a safe working environment for all employees.

Procedures:

Safety Equipment: Provide necessary safety equipment and personal protective gear.

Emergency Procedures: Develop and communicate emergency procedures. **Incident Reporting:** Report and investigate workplace accidents or injuries. 7.2 Client Safety Policy Statement:

Heartfelt Care Services Limited prioritizes the safety and well-being of its clients.

Procedures:

Risk Assessment: Conduct risk assessments at client locations.

Staff Training: Train staff on client safety protocols.

Monitoring: Regularly monitor and evaluate client safety practices.

Technology and Data Management

8.1 IT Security Policy

Statement:

Heartfelt Care Services Limited ensures the security of its IT systems and data.

Procedures:

Access Control: Implement access control measures to restrict unauthorized access. **Data Encryption:** Encryption is used to protect sensitive data.

Backup: Ensure regular backups are conducted to minimize the risk of data loss

Security Training: Provide IT security training to employees.

8.2 Data Management Policy

Statement:

Heartfelt Care Services Limited maintains accurate and secure data management practices.

Procedures:

Data Collection: Collect data with consent and for legitimate purposes only.

Data Storage: Store data securely and limit access to authorized personnel.

Data Retention: Retain data only for as long as necessary and in compliance with regulations. **Data Disposal:** Dispose of data securely when no longer needed.

Quality Assurance

Policy Statement:

Heartfelt Care Services Limited is committed to maintaining high standards of service quality.

Procedures:

Quality Standards: Establish clear quality standards and benchmarks.

Monitoring: Regularly monitor service delivery against quality standards.

Feedback: Collect feedback from clients and employees to identify areas for improvement.

Ongoing Enhancement: Apply updates and modifications informed by feedback and monitoring results.

Review and Revision

Policy Statement:

Heartfelt Care Services Limited regularly reviews and updates its policies and procedures.

Procedures:

Review Schedule: Conduct a policy and procedure review annually.

Revisions: Update policies and procedures based on regulatory changes, feedback, and best practices.

Communication: Communicate any changes to employees and stakeholders promptly.

Terms and Conditions for Heartfelt Care Services Limited

Introduction

Welcome to Heartfelt Care Services Limited Here's a rephrased version:

"These Terms and Conditions ("Terms") explain the provisions and expectations that govern your relationship with us. "

Heartfelt Care Services Limited ("Company," "we," "us," or "our"). By accessing our services, you confirm your acceptance and agreement to comply with these Terms. **Definitions**

Client: Any individual or entity that engages the services of Heartfelt Care Services Limited. Candidate: Any individual placed or employed by Heartfelt Care Services Limited.

Services: Recruitment, employment placement, and care services provided by Heartfelt Care Services Limited. **Services** Service Description:

Heartfelt Care Services Limited provides recruitment and employment placement services specializing in healthcare staffing. We source, screen, and place qualified candidates with clients and may also directly employ staff for home care services.

Client Obligations Accurate Information:

Clients must provide accurate and complete information about their staffing requirements and work environment.

Compliance: Clients must follow all relevant laws and regulations, including employment, health, and safety.

Payment:

Clients agree to pay all fees for the services as specified in the service agreement. **Candidate Obligations** Accurate Information:

Candidates must provide accurate and complete information regarding their qualifications, experience, and availability.

Compliance:

Candidates must comply with all applicable laws, regulations, and professional standards while performing their duties.

Fees and Payment

Fee Structure:

The service agreement with each Client will detail the fees for recruitment and placement services. Fees may be Calculated as a percentage of the candidate's annual salary or as a fixed fee per placement.

- **Invoices**: Invoices will be issued weekly at the end of each week in which personnel have been provided. The Client agrees to pay the Agency within seven days from the invoice date.

- **Late Payments**: In the event of delayed payment, a late fee of **3% per week will** be applied. If payments are delayed by more than 14 days, the Agency retains the right to suspend personnel provision until outstanding amounts are settled.

3.3 **Refund Policy:**

If a placed candidate leaves the Client's employment within_________________________ days, the Agency will provide a replacement at no additional charge or refund _____________________% of the placement fee. No refund is applicable for short-term placements once the candidate has started the assignment.

Responsibilities of the Parties

4.1 Agency Responsibilities:

- Source and screen candidates based on the Client's requirements.
- Verify candidate qualifications, experience, and references.
- Ensure candidates are informed about the job description and requirements.

4.2 Client Responsibilities:

- Provide accurate and complete job descriptions and requirements.
- Notify the Agency of any changes to the job requirements.
- Conduct final interviews and make the hiring decision.
- Inform the Agency promptly if a placed candidate leaves within the refund period.

Confidentiality

Confidential Information:

Both parties agree to uphold the confidentiality of any information exchanged during the relationship. Services are private and not disclosed to third parties without prior consent.

Data Protection:

We follow all applicable data protection laws, including GDPR. For more information, kindly refer to our Privacy Policy.

HEARTFELT CARE SERVICES LIMITED CONFIDENTIALITY POLICY

Confidentiality Policy

Purpose: To provide information and guidance to staff on all areas of maintaining confidentiality.

Scope: This policy applies to all communication and information, whether verbal or written which is not in the public domain. It contains information and guidance from legislation and from relevant bodies that all staff are expected to adhere to including:

- Health and Social Care Act 2008 (Regulated Activities) Regulations 2014

- Data Protection Act (2018)

- Human Rights Act (1998)

- Oher relevant guidance

Managers should check guidance from relevant bodies on a regular basis to ensure they are up to date with the latest information about confidentiality and will amend this policy accordingly.

Staff are expected to adhere to this legislation through implementation of the policy.

Policy

- **Heartfelt Care services Limited** respects the privacy of all service users and recognises that individuals are different in the way they live their lives. Staff are bound by **Heartfelt Care services Limited**'s confidentiality policy. Any staff member who has access to privileged information enters an obligation to keep such information confidential during and after employment with **Heartfelt Care services Limited**. This also means not using confidential information for illegitimate purposes.

- Staff will not divulge to third parties matters confidential to **Heartfelt Care services Limited** or service users (whether covered by this policy) without written explicit authorisation from both **Heartfelt Care services Limited** and the service user and with clear explanations of why the information needs to be shared.

- Where it is agreed to share information, this will only be shared with others on a need-to-know basis.

- Where **Heartfelt Care services Limited** discovers an actual or potential breach of this policy, it will act quickly with service users to seek appropriate redress to prevent further damage to the service user or **Heartfelt Care services Limited**'s reputation. Make sure you cross reference this policy with your GDPR policy as regards any breaches.

- Staff who divulge confidential information to third parties about service users will be held personally liable for any legal action taken against them by the service user.

- Except where otherwise agreed, all material, data, information etc. collected during the staff member's employment will remain in the possession **Heartfelt Care services Limited** or the service user.

Liability

Limitation of Liability:

Heartfelt Care Services Limited's Liability for any claims arising out of or in connection with Liability for the services will be restricted to the total fees the Client has paid for the services provided in question.

Indemnity:

Clients agree to indemnify and hold Heartfelt Care Services Limited harmless from any claims, damages, or losses arising from the Client's breach of these Terms or applicable laws.

Termination

Termination by Client: Clients can end the service agreement by giving 30 days written notice. All pending fees for services provided up to the termination date will be due.

Termination by Company:

We reserve the right to terminate the service agreement immediately if the Client breaches these Terms or fails to pay fees when due.

Dispute Resolution

Governing Law:

Governing Law: These Terms shall be interpreted and enforced in line with the laws of England and Wales.

Dispute Resolution:

Any conflicts originating from or associated with these Terms will be settled through negotiation. If the dispute cannot be resolved through negotiation, it shall be referred to mediation or arbitration as mutually agreed by the parties.

Amendments

Changes to Terms:

We reserve the right to amend these Terms at any time. Clients will be notified of any significant updates and continued use of our services after such notification constitutes acceptance of the new Terms.

Miscellaneous

Entire Agreement:

These Terms and any service these agreements represent the entire understanding between the parties and override any previous agreements or understandings.

Severability:

If any provision of these Terms is found Should any provision be found invalid or unenforceable, the other provisions shall remain fully operative clauses will continue to be fully effective." Waiver:

No term or condition will be considered a further or ongoing waiver of that term or any other term. Contact Information: If you have any inquiries or concerns about these Terms, feel free to reach out to us at:"

Heartfelt Care Services Limited

Email: info@hcslteam.co.uk

Privacy Policy for Heartfelt Care Services Limited

Heartfelt Care Services Limited ("e," s," or "our"). Our commitment is to protect your privacy. This Privacy Policy explains how we gather, manage and share your personal information. We collect, utilize, and share your data by the UK General Data Protection Regulation (GDPR).

Information We Collect

We collect the following types of personal data:

- Personal Information: Your name, email address, phone number, home address, and more.

- **Employment Information**: Job title (e.g., Support Worker, Care Assistant), work experience, qualifications, training certificates, DBS checks, and references.

- **Sensitive Data**: Health information when required (e.g., fitness for work), ethnic background (optional), and any other information relevant to the recruitment and employment process.

How We Use Your Information

We use your data to:

- Facilitate recruitment processes for Support Worker and Care Assistant roles.
- Manage job applications and employment placements.
- Conduct background checks, including DBS, for compliance with health and social care regulations.
- Communicate with you regarding job opportunities or necessary updates.
- Ensure legal and regulatory compliance within the healthcare sector.

How We Share Your Information

We may share your information with:

- Prospective employers for job placement purposes.
- Regulatory bodies, as required by law (e.g., Care Quality Commission,
Disclosure and Barring Service).
- Service providers such as payroll processors or HR software providers assist with business operations. We do not sell or trade your personal information to third parties.

Data Security

We are committed to protecting your data and employing suitable technical and organizational safeguards to prevent unauthorized access, disclosure, or loss

Your Rights

You have the right to:

•	Request access to your data.

•	Request correction of inaccurate or incomplete information.

•	Request deletion of your data under certain circumstances.

•	Withdraw consent is required to process your data at any time.

To exercise your rights, feel free to contact us at Info@hcslteam.co.uk

Changes to This Privacy Policy

This Privacy Policy may be updated periodically. Any modifications will be made available on our website."

Should you have any questions or concerns regarding this policy, please get in touch with us at 00447542732009.

Non-Discrimination Policy

Non-Discrimination Policy for Heartfelt Care Services Limited

Heartfelt Care Services Limited promotes an inclusive and diverse workplace for all Support Workers and Care Assistants. We strictly prohibit discrimination based on the following:

•	Race, ethnicity, or nationality

- Gender, gender identity, or gender expression
- Sexual orientation
- Age
- Disability
- Religion or belief
- Marital status or family status
- Pregnancy or maternity

Scope of the Policy

This policy applies to all employees, job applicants, clients, and contractors associated with Heartfelt Care Services Limited. It covers all aspects of employment, including:

- Recruitment and selection for Support Worker and Care Assistant positions
- Training and development opportunities
- Work conditions and benefits
- Employees must protect clients' confidentiality, including personal data, medical records, and any sensitive information encountered during their duties.
- Breaches of confidentiality may result in disciplinary action, including termination of employment.

Training and Development

- Employees must participate in mandatory training sessions to equip them with the skills and knowledge required to carry out their duties effectively and safely.

•	Opportunities for additional training and development will be provided to promote professional growth.

Equal Opportunity

• Heartfelt Care Services Limited is committed to providing all employees and applicants equal employment opportunities. We do not tolerate discrimination and provide fair treatment based on merit and performance.

Grievances

• Employees are encouraged to address grievances openly with their supervisor. They may escalate the issue to HR or management if it remains unresolved.

Termination

Employment with Heartfelt Care Services Limited is at-will, meaning the employee or the company may end the employment relationship at any time, with or without reason, by UK employment laws.

HEARTFELT CARE SERVICES LIMITED CONSENT POLICY

Consent Policy

Purpose: To provide information and guidance to staff on all aspects of gaining consent.

Scope: Contains information and guidance from legislation and from relevant bodies that all staff are expected to adhere to, including:

- Mental Capacity Act (2005)
- Mental Capacity Act (2005) Code of Practice
- Health and Social Care Act 2008 (Regulated Activities) Regulations 2014 - Regulation 11 (Need for consent)

Managers should check guidance from relevant bodies regularly to ensure they are up to date with the latest information about consent and will amend this policy and its procedures accordingly.

Staff are expected to adhere to this legislation by implementing the policy and procedures.

Consent is a formal acceptance from service users to accept the care and treatment assessed, planned and offered.

Consent procedures

1. Training requirements

All staff will receive training on how to manage consent. Training will include:

- The legislation and how this might affect staff.
- What does this policy and procedures expect of staff?
- Define the different types of consent and when they are appropriate.
- How to identify whether a service user might not have the capacity to consent.
- Make sure people have all the required information to help them make an informed decision and know what this might include.
- How to ensure people give consent voluntarily.
- What to do if a person can't decide.
- Documentation required when dealing with consent and how staff should complete this.
- Care planning requirements.
- Staff roles and responsibilities.
- How to review consent.

Gaining consent

Consent will be required for all aspects of care and treatment, although this doesn't have to be in writing, provided a contemporaneous record is made of the consent.

The following consent is required to be in writing:

- Entering or leaving the service.
- Agreeing to the care/service plan.
- The use of specialist equipment such as hoists or other equipment arranged to be delivered to the service user's home.
- The use of equipment that might be restrictive (according to Dolls), such as bed rails.

- Specialist treatments include intravenous infusions, syringe drivers, and PEG feeding systems.
- Participation in social activities and outings.
- Participation in projects or research activities.

All other consent can be given verbally or implied, although staff should always obtain the service user's consent and document their response.

Staff should ensure that the service user makes the decision voluntarily and is not under duress from clinicians, family, or others to decide they do not really want to make.

1. Testing capacity

Staff should follow the four steps below when testing capacity. They should be able to assess whether the service user meets the criteria for each step.

1. Does the service user understand the decision they must make and why?
2. Does the service user realise what will happen if they do or don't decide?
3. Can the service user retain the information long enough to decide whether to make the decision? Can the service user convey their decision verbally, nonverbally, or with the help of another professional, such as a speech therapist?

1. Providing information

Staff should make sure people have the following information with which to help them make an informed decision about their care and treatment:

- Information about their condition and prognosis.

- Information about the signs and symptoms they might experience.
- Information about the care and treatment proposed.
- Information about the benefits of the care and treatment proposed.
- Information about the risks associated with the care and treatment proposed.
- The answers to other information requested.

In addition, staff should ensure this information is understandable, considering the person's communication abilities, language, culture, and religion.

1.   Best interest decisions

If there is no lasting power of attorney to make decisions, or the power of attorney needs the help of professionals to make a complex range of decisions, a 'best interest' meeting will be set up.

The meetings should:

- Encourage participation from the service user where possible.
- Identify the issues where the service user cannot decide and separate these from those decisions they can make.
- Find out what the service user might have done had they been able to decide for themselves. It might include:

-

-

- Reviewing their past actions, wishes, behaviours and habits.

- Taking account of any cultural, religious, social or political beliefs and values.
- Avoid discrimination.
- Withhold making the decision, if possible, if the lack of capacity is temporary.
- Consult others who may be able to provide insight into the person's past wishes, values, and beliefs. It might include relatives, friends, carers, advocates, solicitors, people with power of attorney, doctors, professional staff and even a court-appointed person.
- Decide about the person's best interest that doesn't restrict their rights.
- Find out whether the person has a valid advance decision to refuse treatment. If so, the 'best interest' panel cannot overturn this.

Managers should document meetings. This will include keeping a record of how the panel decided the person's best interests and why, who was present at the meetings, and what issues the panel considered when making the decision.

This record should remain on the person's file. Managers should update the service user plan and inform all staff of their responsibilities in caring for and treating the person.

1.   **Care planning**

The care plan should be updated to ensure staff ask whether the service user consents to care and treatment at this visit and to each task involved. Staff should record consent in the care records. Staff should complete this procedure in conjunction with their usual care planning requirements.

2.   Regular review

Consent should be reviewed regularly alongside all other care and reaffirmed (in writing if initially given this way). Managers should complete this procedure in conjunction with their standard review requirements.

3.   Record keeping

Staff will record consent in the notes as per the care/service plan as part of their normal record-keeping requirements.

HEARTFELT CARE SERVICES LIMITED DISCIPLINARY POLICY AND PROCEDURE

Disciplinary Policy

Purpose: To provide information and guidance on how to discipline staff.

Policy: Heartfelt Care Services Limited understand that from time to time, managers may need to discipline staff due to the following:

- Performance reasons: The staff member is unable to perform the job even after being given the appropriate support, training, leadership, and work systems to enable this.
- Conduct reasons: The staff member has fallen below the expected levels of conduct, e.g., poor timekeeping, unauthorised absences, discrimination, bullying, or harassment.
- Gross misconduct, such as:
- A breach of confidentiality.
- Theft, e.g. of the organisation's, another staff member or a service user's property.
- Working for another organisation whilst on a leave of absence without prior consent.
- Unprovoked physical violence, abusive language or actions that are hostile or disrespectful

towards a manager, another staff member, service user, family member or carer.

•   Ignoring health and safety procedures or creating or putting oneself or others in an unsafe work situation.

•   Unauthorised use or distribution of company information.

•   Violating the organisation's equal opportunity, harassment or whistleblowing policies.

•   Improper personal behaviour, e.g. working whilst under the influence of drugs or alcohol.

•   Malicious damage to the organisation's or service user's property or premises.

Heartfelt Care Services Limited is committed to investigating and resolving disciplinary problems early before they affect the safety of the organisation, service users, and staff.

Scope: This policy contains information and guidance from:

•   Akas Code of Practice 1: Disciplinary and grievance procedures (2015)

•   Akas Guide: Discipline and grievances at work (2019)

Managers should check guidance from relevant bodies regularly to ensure they are up to date with the latest information about disciplinary proceedings and amend this policy and its procedures accordingly. Staff are expected to adhere to this legislation through the implementation of its policy and procedures. We will treat all disciplinary issues in confidence in the first instance.

The Registered Manager will arrange for the appropriate personnel to handle the disciplinary process.

Disciplinary Procedure

1.   <insert Name of manager> will establish the facts of the disciplinary problem and investigate to collect evidence of poor performance or conduct. Heartfelt Care Services Limited will decide whether to suspend the staff member while carrying out the investigations and following hearings. <insert Name of manager> will then inform the staff member of the need for a meeting to respond to the problem. It will be in writing.

1.   <insert Name of manager> will invite the staff member to a meeting to discuss the problem, giving them all the time and venue details to enable them to attend the hearing. The staff member can bring a colleague or a trade union representative to the hearing.

1.   <insert Name of manager> will hold the meeting with the staff member to explain the performance or conduct problem and allow the staff member to put forward their side of the problem. Any representatives accompanying staff should not answer questions on the staff member's behalf nor prevent the staff member from answering questions.

1.   <insert Name of manager> will decide whether further action is justified. Unsatisfactory performance or misconduct will be punished by:

- [Verbal or written warning – for a first offence.
- Final written warning – if more serious.

- Dismissal – with or without notice – depending on the seriousness of the circumstances (e.g. with notice for redundancy, without notice for gross misconduct)]

Provide staff with an opportunity to appeal against the result.

1. <insert Name of manager> will allow staff to appeal against the result. Appeal hearings will take place within <5 working days>). They will be heard by <insert Name of a different manager> to ensure impartiality. As for the initial hearing, the staff member will be given all the time and venue details to enable them to attend it. Once again, the staff member can bring a colleague or a trade union representative.

1. The staff member can offer additional evidence not heard in the first hearing. <insert Name of manager> will explain to the staff member that their decision is final.

1. <insert Name of manager> will decide whether there is new evidence to overturn the original decision or whether to retain the original decision. <insert Name of manager>will inform the staff member of the meeting outcome in writing. The staff member must consider whether they are happy with the response or, if they are not satisfied with the result, whether to take this to a Tribunal.

Promotions or career advancement

Harassment and Bullying

We do not tolerate any form of harassment or bullying, including inappropriate behaviour towards any individual based on their race, gender, age, or other personal characteristics. Discrimination or harassment will be addressed with the utmost seriousness and investigated promptly.

Reporting and Accountability

Employees, including Support Workers and Care Assistants, who believe they have been subject to discrimination or harassment are encouraged to report the incident to management or HR without fear of retaliation. Heartfelt Care Services Limited will take appropriate disciplinary action, up to and including dismissal, against individuals found violating this policy.

Heartfelt Care Services Limited is an equal opportunity employer and adheres to all local laws regarding non-discrimination.

General Employment Guidelines

General Employment Guidelines for Heartfelt Care Services Limited

Heartfelt Care Services Limited employs support workers and care assistants responsible for delivering high-quality care and support to clients. These guidelines define the expectations and duties of all employees to ensure a safe, professional, and respectful working environment.

Employee Conduct

•	All employees, including Support Workers and Care Assistants, must maintain professionalism, respect, and integrity when representing Heartfelt Care Services Limited and working with clients.

•	Employees must maintain client confidentiality and protect sensitive client information through company policies and data protection laws.

Attendance and Punctuality

• Employees are expected to be punctual and maintain regular attendance. Employees who cannot attend a scheduled shift must notify their manager as early as possible.

Frequent unexcused absences or late arrivals may lead to disciplinary action, including termination of employment.

Dress Code

•	Employees must wear appropriate attire for their role, including a uniform or specified clothing, to ensure safety and hygiene in care settings.

•	Support Workers and Care Assistants must comply with health and safety regulations related to personal protective equipment (PPE), especially when working with vulnerable clients.

Health and Safety

•	All employees must follow the company and safety policies created to uphold a safe working environment for themselves and the clients they support.

- Any accidents, injuries, or safety hazards must be reported immediately to management.

Use of Company Resources

- Employees are expected to use company resources, including equipment, mobile devices, or other materials, responsibly and solely for work-related purposes.
- Misuse of resources may result in disciplinary action. Confidentiality

HEARTFELT CARE SERVICES LIMITED FALLS POLICY AND PROCEDURE

Purpose: To provide information and guidance to staff on preventing and managing falls.

Scope: Contains information and guidance from legislation and guidance relevant bodies that all staff must adhere to, including:

- Care Quality Commission – Health and Social Care Act 2008 (Regulated Activities) Regulations 2014 – Regulation 12 – Safe Care and Treatment and Regulation 15 – Premises and equipment.
- Health and Safety at Work Act 1974.
- Management of Health and Safety at Work Regulations 1999.

Managers should regularly check guidance from relevant bodies to ensure they are up to date with the latest information about consent and amend this policy and its procedures accordingly.

Staff should adhere to this legislation by implementing the policy and procedures.

Procedures

Preventing Falls

Staff will use the standard risk assessment process to:

Identify the risk of falling, which will include:

- Assessing the person to identify risk factors that might lead to falls.
- Assessing the environmental and other risk factors from within the home that might lead to falls.

Decide what interventions you need to implement to prevent falls from occurring and put these systems in place.

Record the interventions on the care/service plan so that staff know what they should do for each service user.

Record falls using the Data Recording Sheet and evaluate falls regularly to monitor success.

Managing Falls

- If you find someone has fallen, follow your accident and emergency policy to ensure the person's safety and well-being.
- Review any falls that occur to ensure that you have identified all risks and that the identified measures were taken to prevent the fall.
- Instigate any fall management measures identified following a fall.

Reviewing falls

Using the data recording sheet, carry out a review every <insert timeframe> months as a means of improving the fall prevention programme. Complete a report to include:

- How many falls are occurring?
- Why have the falls occurred?
- What caused the falls, and could they have been identified?
- What risk measures were in place (if any)?
- Could anything be done to prevent the fall?

- Are there similarities between the times, locations or activities that can be drawn on to avoid further falls?
- Are interventions working?

HEARTFELT CARE SERVICES LIMITED FIRST AID POLICY AND PROCEDURES

First Aid Policy and Procedures

Purpose: To provide information and guidance to staff on how to take the appropriate action when first aid is needed.

Policy: Heartfelt Care Services Limited will provide appropriate first aid training to help staff give first aid when needed. If staff feel anxious about providing first aid, they should inform their line manager immediately. The manager will then provide extra training and support.

Scope: This policy contains information and guidance from:

Health and Social Care Act 2008 (Regulated Activities) Regulations 2014

Care Quality Commission (Registration) Regulations 2009

The Health and Safety (First Aid) Regulations 1981

Care Certificate 2015

Managers should check guidance from relevant bodies annually. They must then amend this policy and its procedures to ensure they are up to date with the latest information about first aid.

Staff are expected to adhere to this legislation by implementing the policy and procedures.

First Aid Procedures

1.   Ensure you have enough trained personnel on duty

First aiders are workforce staff who have volunteered to take on the role. Those staff providing care are all required to have basic life support training to assist service users in an emergency.

Organisations with at most 25 staff are required to have one appointed person in place. This person will look after first-aid equipment and facilities and call the emergency services when necessary.

Organisations with 25–50 staff must have at least one first-aider trained in emergency first aid at work (EFAW).

Organisations with over 50 staff must have at least one first-aider trained in first aid at work (FAW) for every 100 employed.

The appointed person can be someone other than a qualified first aider.

Heartfelt Care Services Limited will indemnify any staff member who assists an employee who becomes ill or is injured.

1.   Keep the first aid box up to date.

Following the first aid needs assessment, a list of first-aid equipment for the first-aid box(es) will be provided inside the box.

The first-aid kit(s) will be kept <insert location> so that all staff know where to find this.

The appointed person will check the first aid box weekly and ensure its contents are up-to-date and fully stocked.

Provide first aid in an emergency.

Staff trained in this will provide first aid using the steps below.

Step 1: Check the surroundings. It is to identify and remove any hazards that might jeopardise the safety of the service user and others in the surrounding area. Staff should not put themselves in danger by doing this.

Step 2: Check whether the person is responsive. For example, ask them to open their eyes. If they don't, tap their shoulder or pinch their small fingernail to come back or ear lobe to see if they respond.

Step 3 – Provide the following care:

A = Airway—Check that the person's airway is open. If they are responsive, they may be able to do this for themselves. If they can't or are unresponsive, remove any obvious obstructions and tilt their heads back to open the airway.

B = Breathing – Check that the person is breathing. If they are breathing, that's good; put them into the recovery position. If the person is not breathing, staff may need to clear the airway of any obstruction and open it if they have not already done so. If the person still doesn't start breathing after this, staff should call 999 and commence CPR.

C = Circulation—If the person is bleeding, staff must stop the bleeding by applying compression to the wound. If it is a limb, they can also raise it upwards above the level of the person's heart (if this won't cause further injury).

Step 4: Check whether the person is in shock and treat this by laying the person down and raising their feet above the height of their head. Signs of shock include a pale face, cold and clammy, fast and shallow breathing or a quick, fluttery pulse.

Step 5: Stay with the person until additional help arrives, e.g. ambulance, GP, etc.

Record accidents and incidents

All accidents, however minor, must be recorded in the accident and incident book.

The accident and incident book will be kept <insert location>.

The staff member dealing with the accident is responsible for completing the entry in the accident book as soon as possible after the event.

The registered manager must be informed immediately when an accident results in hospital admission or an inability to continue work.

HEARTFELT CARE SERVICES LIMITED DRUG AND ALCOHOL ABUSE POLICY AND PROCEDURES

Drug and Alcohol Abuse

Policy and Procedures

Purpose: To provide information to your staff on your expectations concerning their use of drugs and alcohol.

Policy: Heartfelt Care Services Limited is committed to keeping service users safe from staff under the influence of drugs and alcohol. It expects employees to follow the procedures contained within this policy to make sure staff always keep service users safe.

Scope: This policy contains information and guidance from legislation and from relevant bodies that includes, but is not exclusive to:

- Road Traffic Act (1988) – it is an offence to drive under the influence of alcohol and drugs. Many home care staff drive to their service users.

- The Health and Social Care Act 2008 (Regulated Activities) Regulations 2014 – Safe Care and Treatment (Regulation 12); Safeguarding service users from abuse and improper treatment (Regulation 13); Fit and proper persons employed (Regulation 19). The CQC expect your staff to be of good character and provide safe care to your service users.

- Misuse of Drugs Act (1971) – makes it illegal to use Controlled Drugs without a valid prescription. Decide whether legitimate use of this medication will affect the service user's safety.

- Human Medicines Regulations 2012 – make using a prescription-only medication without a prescription illegal. Once again, decide whether legitimate use of this medication will affect the service user's safety.

- The Health and Safety at Work Act (1974) and The Management of Health and Safety at Work Regulations (1999) – expect you to provide safe care. Staff cannot do this safely if they are under the influence of drugs or alcohol.

- Provision and Use of Work Equipment Regulations (1998) – expects staff to use equipment safely. Being under the influence of drugs/alcohol may compromise this requirement.

This policy and procedures apply to all Heartfelt Care Services Limited staff.

The Registered Manager should regularly check guidance from relevant bodies to ensure they are up to date with drug and alcohol legislation and will amend this policy and its procedures accordingly. Staff are expected to adhere to this legislation by implementing the policy and procedures.

Procedures   **Staff Recruitment**

Heartfelt Care Services Limited expects registered managers to take responsibility for recruiting the right person for the role. The company will make its position on drug and alcohol abuse clear to prospective staff during the recruitment process. It will include outlining the policy and procedures about drug/alcohol abuse.

If Disclosure and Barring Checks (DBC) identify past drug and alcohol abuse, Heartfelt Care Services Limited will decide whether the person is sufficiently rehabilitated that the drug/alcohol abuse does not breach this policy and procedures.

Company Expectations

Heartfelt Care Services Limited operates a [identify what your policy is and add this here – you will need to amend the rest of the policy in line with this] policy. [When identifying what your policy should be, you should consider the following:

• Should you have a blanket ban on drugs/alcohol for all staff? It would include deciding whether this applies to lunchtimes, mainly if staff are unpaid during their lunch breaks.

•   Should you decide not to ban staff from drinking alcohol, expect them to maintain professional conduct during working hours.

• Whether you restrict staff from reporting on duty within certain hours of taking drugs/drinking alcohol.

• Will you allow alcohol consumption at limited times, e.g., leaving parties, training events, or entertaining clients (mainly if this is outside regular working hours).?

It means no staff should [ever be under the influence of drugs/alcohol] whenever carrying out their role for Heartfelt Care Services Limited.

If a staff member is involved in recreational drug/alcohol use, it is their responsibility to ensure that these are no longer in their system when attending work.

Disciplinary Action

If a member of staff is struggling with drug/alcohol abuse, Heartfelt Care Services Limited will give the person support, if possible, to overcome this. However, the health and safety of service users are paramount, and a staff member will not be allowed to continue working if it is thought that their actions might endanger others.

If a staff member is suspected of drug/alcohol use contrary to your policy, they will be expected to undergo a test before continuing with their work.

However, if Heartfelt Care Services Limited finds a staff member to be [under the influence of drugs/alcohol whilst at work—add in your requirement], this will be gross misconduct. In this instance, Heartfelt Care Services Limited will follow the usual disciplinary procedure. The outcome will likely be staff dismissal.

Review

Heartfelt Care Services Limited will treat all incidents relating to actual and alleged drug/alcohol misuse in confidence.

However, if Heartfelt Care Services Limited is concerned that a crime has been committed, this will be reported to the police, e.g. using or selling Controlled Drugs on the premises or driving under the influence of drugs/alcohol.

An annual review of this policy will make sure it is up to date with current legislation.

HEARTFELT CARE SERVICES LIMITED FOOD SAFETY POLICY AND PROCEDURES

Food Safety Policy

Purpose: To provide staff information and guidance on handling food safely.

Policy: Heartfelt Care Services Limited is committed to keeping service users safe from food-borne infection when providing food services to them. It expects employees to follow the procedures contained within this policy to make sure staff keep food free from disease and cross-contamination when shopping, storing, preparing and cooking food on behalf of the service user.

Scope: This policy contains information and guidance from legislation and from relevant bodies that include:

- Food Safety Act (1990)

- Food Hygiene (England) Regulations 2006 (as amended) and Regulation (EC) No. 852/2004
- Guidance about compliance: Essential standards of quality and safety (2010) - Outcome 5: Meeting nutritional needs

The [Registered Manager / Other Manager] is responsible for implementing and reviewing this policy and will regularly check guidance from relevant bodies to ensure Heartfelt Care Services Limited is updated with the latest food safety legislation. [Registered Manager / Other Manager] will amend this policy and its procedures accordingly. Staff are expected to adhere to this legislation by implementing the policy and procedures and report any concerns to this person immediately after the event.

Food Safety Procedures

Food hygiene requirements

Heartfelt Care Services Limited expects staff to wash their hands in hand hot water and soap, rinse them thoroughly and dry them on paper towels or a clean hand towel:

- Before and after handling food.
- In between touching raw and cooked food.
- After handling food waste.
- After cleaning.
- After blowing their nose, going to the toilet, touching pets, touching their hair, etc.

Any staff handling food should avoid wearing the following:

- False nails.
- Nail varnish.
- Jewellery when preparing food.

Staff should cover the wound with a blue plaster if they cut themselves.

Heartfelt Care Services Limited expects staff to wear gloves and an apron over their work clothes when preparing food. Long hair should be tied back.

1.   Managing Staff Sickness

Staff must not handle food if they have an infected wound, skin infection, or sores. If staff have vomited or have diarrhoea, they must stay away from the service for 48 hours after the last about of sickness. When reporting sickness, follow the Sickness Absence Policy.

On returning to work, staff must inform their manager of this condition or illness.

Shopping requirements

If shopping for the service user, Heartfelt Care Services Limited expects staff to adhere to the following when shopping:

- Buy frozen or refrigerated food at the end of the shop.
- Take note of 'use-by' dates on food to ensure it lasts long enough to be eaten.
- Keep raw and cooked foods separate in the trolley and pack these into bags when packing.
- Pack food that can be damaged easily at the top of your bags.
- Keep food away from car heaters when transporting it to the service user.
- Frozen food or anything that needs to be refrigerated should be put away as soon as possible, mainly if the weather is hot and within two hours of purchase.

Storage arrangements

When putting any shopping away for the service user, Heartfelt Care Services Limited expects staff to adhere to the following arrangements:

•	Label food by entering the date of purchase onto sticky labels provided and attaching this to the foodstuff.

•	Take account of 'use-by' dates when storing food.

•	Store raw foods away from other foods in the fridge and in sealed containers. For example, raw meats (even packaged) can be stored on the bottom shelves of the refrigerator or freezer, along with other products on the shelves above.

Prepare food safely, including cleaning equipment and surfaces.

When preparing food for the service user, Heartfelt Care Services Limited expects staff to adhere to the following arrangements:

•	Adhere to the above food hygiene arrangements.

•	Wear PPE such as single-use, disposable gloves, have long hair tied back and wear a material apron.

•	Wash worktops before and after preparing food, mainly after they have been in contact with raw meat, including poultry, raw eggs, fish and vegetables, using the following regime:

•	Pre-clean – to remove crumbs or old food debris.

•	Clean – wash with hot, soapy (detergent) water.

- Rinse – to remove the detergent.
- [Disinfect – with an anti-bacterial spray. Leave on the surface briefly to let it kill bacteria.]
- Wash off – disinfectant with clear, hot water.
- Dry thoroughly.
- It would help if you kept all tools and equipment used to prepare food clean.
- During preparation, keep food covered wherever possible.
- Wash fruit, vegetables and salads in clean water to remove soil, chemicals and insects.
- Defrost frozen food thoroughly before cooking (as instructed).

Cooking food safely

When cooking food for the service user, Heartfelt Care Services Limited expects staff to adhere to the following arrangements:

- Cooked foods (especially meat, such as poultry) should be cooked correctly. See Appendix 1 for ideal cooking temperatures. Check meat temperatures with a food probe and visually ensure no pink meat in foods such as burgers, chicken, sausages, and meat joints.
- If food is chilled and then reheated, it should be piping hot all through. Stir it if possible, to ensure no cool spots (this goes for microwaved food, too).
- Never reheat cooked food more than once.
- Do not leave food on the heat for 2 hours at 63°C or above. After 2 hours, if the service user is not going to eat the food, you must cool it as quickly as possible to 5°C or below and store it in the refrigerator or discard it.

- When heating food in a microwave, ensure the proper containers are used. Then, follow the manufacturer's cooking instructions.
- Food waste should be disposed of quickly and hygienically.

Dealing with Food Poisoning Outbreaks

If two or more cases of the same symptoms occur within a few days of each other, the [Registered Manager / Other Manager] will report this to the environmental health department at your local council.

Review

An annual review of this policy will make sure it is up to date with current legislation.

HEARTFELT CARE SERVICES LIMITED MEDICATION POLICY

Medication Policy

Purpose: To provide information and guidance for staff within HEARTFELT CARE SERVICES LIMITED to enable them to administer medication safely within the organisation.

Policy: This Medication Policy outlines the requirements of HEARTFELT CARE SERVICES LIMITED regarding the administration of medication by its staff. HEARTFELT CARE SERVICES LIMITED must keep service users safe when providing medication services and will always uphold this duty. However, it acknowledges that sometimes things will go wrong. If they do, it expects staff to take the appropriate emergency action to deal with any health issues, report the error correctly, and participate in any activity that will help reduce similar mistakes.

Scope:

This Policy contains information and guidance from legislation and from relevant bodies that all staff are expected to adhere to, including:

Health and Social Care Act 2008 (Regulated Activities) Regulations 2014.

Care Quality Commission (Registration) Regulations 2009.

National Institute for Health and Care Excellence (NICE) Guidance (NG5) 2015 – Medicines optimisation: the safe and effective use of medicines to enable the best possible outcomes.

National Institute for Health and Care Excellence (NICE) Guidance (SC1) 2014 – Managing medicines in care homes.

National Institute for Health and Care Excellence (NICE) Quality standards (QS85) 2015 – Medicines Management in Care Homes.

Whilst this Policy covers all staff employed either temporarily or permanently, full or part-time within <insert Name of Organisation>. Qualified nurses are accountable for their professional practice and must adhere to the Code of Conduct of the Nursing and Midwifery Council (NMC). Those managers who are themselves qualified nurses may be held professionally accountable for upholding the NMC code.

Medication Services:

Staff within HEARTFELT CARE SERVICES LIMITED can prompt, assist, or administer medication depending on the service user's needs. Staff will only give medications orally (tablets or elixir), topically (i.e., creams and lotions), or via instillation (i.e., eye and ear drops) or inhalation (i.e., nebulisers). Staff will not give cytotoxic medication by any route.

Organisational Responsibilities:

HEARTFELT CARE SERVICES LIMITED will:

Provide an up-to-date medication policy and procedures for all staff to work within.

Ensure the service users' medication needs, preferences, and risks are identified, and care planned to meet these.

Provide medication training during induction and regular updates for at least 6 months.

Ensuring staff are competent to give medication safely following training.

Provide medication records to enable staff to keep accurate records regarding medication administration.

Review medication needs and preferences regularly.

Audit medication services 6-monthly.

Maintain the service user's rights to independence, dignity, and choice.

Ensure all records and information about a service user's treatment are kept confidential.

Care Workers' Responsibilities

Care workers will:

Always follow HEARTFELT CARE SERVICES LIMITED's medication policy and procedures.

Attend all medication training sessions as requested.

Refrain from carrying out medication services if they need more confidence and competence.

Inform the line manager of any changes in circumstances to the service user.

Always maintain the service user's rights to dignity and independence.

Keep all information about a service user's medication and treatment confidential.

HEARTFELT CARE SERVICES LIMITED RISK ASSESSMENT POLICY

Risk Assessment Policy and Procedure

Purpose: To outline the information and guidance for staff to follow on how to carry out and implement risk assessments.

Policy: Heartfelt Care Services Limited understand that we must manage the risk to service users, staff and others. However, we recognise that service users have the right to make choices about their lives.

These choices may affect the risks associated with providing their care and support. We are committed to balancing these choices with the associated risks in accordance with legislation and best practice. This process is risk assessment and the following procedure details how we seek to meet our obligations in this respect.

Scope: The legislation and guidance staff must adhere to include:

- Care Quality Commission - Health and Social Care Act 2008 (Regulated Activities) Regulations 2014
- Health and Safety at Work Act 1974
- Management of Health and Safety at Work Regulations 1999
- Health and Safety Executive Guidance
- <Add in others relevant to your Organisation>

Assessment of Risk: Risk assessments are to be carried out by staff with the skills, knowledge, and experience to assess risk and determine how the service works.

Definitions

Hazard: Anything that can cause someone harm. It might be a piece of equipment, such as a hoist, an organism, an infection, or how someone works, such as not leaving a walking frame within reach.

Risk: The likelihood that the hazards identified will lead to harm and the damage the hazard could cause.

Reasonably practicable: The Health and Safety Executive (HSE) defines this as 'balancing the level of risk against the measures needed to control the real risk in terms of money, time or trouble. It means that the time and cost of reducing the risk should not outweigh the risk itself.

Reasonably foreseeable: This means that you could reasonably predict something might happen in a given circumstance.

<Add in any other definitions relevant to your Organisation>

Procedure

Step 1. Identify the hazards

Identify hazards within the Organisation in the following ways:

- Use equality legislation to identify areas of risk.
- Walk around the workplace and office to see what hazards can be identified.
- Ask staff about hazards they have noticed in their work area.
- Use accident and incident books, complaints, suggestions and other records to identify hazards that have caused injury within the last [add in time] months.

It should occur every <add in several months> or immediately when hazards are identified.

Use a Risk Assessment Form to identify hazards.

Step 2. Decide who might be harmed and how

Identify the people whom the hazard might harm. As well as staff, the service user and their family or visitors pay particular attention to the following groups of people:

- New members of staff.
- Young or junior members of staff.
- Temporary staff.
- Volunteers.
- Expectant mothers.
- Older members of staff.
- People with disabilities.
- Lone workers.
- Contractors.

Add these to the Risk Assessment Form.

Step 3. Evaluate the risks and decide on precautions

Identify how likely and how severe any harm might be to the person. Then, the level of risk will be worked out using a risk identification table.

How to Assess the Likelihood of Harm Occurring

Assess the likelihood of the hazard causing a risk to the person using the definitions below:

Highly likely: The hazard is expected to cause harm because it occurs regularly, e.g. several times a day or each time the activity occurs.

Moderately likely: The hazard is only moderately likely to cause harm because the hazard only arises occasionally, such as once a month or intermittently.

Not very likely: The hazard is seldom expected to cause harm, as it only arises once or twice a year.

How to Assess the Severity of Harm that Might be Caused

Define the severity of harm as follows:

Severely harmful: The hazard may cause death or significant injury, such as loss of a limb or illness that causes long-term disability that might result in long-term care or hospital treatment.

Moderately harmful: The hazard might cause injuries or illnesses, resulting in short-term or temporary disability and short hospital stays or visits.

Slightly harmful: The hazard might cause minor injuries or illnesses that need first aid treatment.

Now plot these on a Risk Identification Table to determine the level of risk and the type of control measures needed to reduce it.

Add the level of risk to a Risk Assessment Form.

Decide upon control measures to reduce or prevent the risk from occurring using the following order:

1. Removing the hazard altogether.
2. Try a less risky option.
3. Prevent access to the hazard.
4. Organise work to reduce exposure to the hazard.
5. Provide personal protective equipment (PPE).
6. Provide safe systems of work.

Add these to a Risk Assessment Form.

Step 4. Record your findings and implement them.

Complete all forms in full, including the control measures, and add these to the care plan where necessary.

Ensure that any measures such as specific care, rewriting policies or procedures, or staff training are carried out.

Step 5. Review your assessment and update it if necessary

Review risk assessments <each year, or however often you choose> or when the following occurs:

- Work practices have changed.
- The service is reorganised.
- Staff have changed.
- The service user's condition has changed.
- A new piece of equipment is introduced.
- A service user loses a carer who has supported them.

Add reviews to a Risk Assessment Form and any additional control measures identified.

About Heartfelt Care Services Limited

Heartfelt Care Services Limited is a recruitment and employment agency based in the United Kingdom dedicated to delivering exceptional staffing solutions in the healthcare and retail sectors. The agency was founded with a vision to connect compassionate, skilled professionals with organizations in need of reliable, high-quality staff. Specializing in temporary and permanent placements, Heartfelt Care Services Limited works closely with care homes, hospitals, clinics, and retail businesses to ensure that workforce needs are met seamlessly. The agency is committed to empowering its clients and candidates by fostering strong partnerships, delivering tailored staffing solutions, and ensuring compliance with industry standards.

From managing short-term placements to offering emergency staffing and comprehensive training services, Heartfelt Care Services Limited is more than just a staffing provider—it is a trusted partner in workforce management. The agency's mission is to uphold the highest standards of care and service, helping clients and candidates thrive in a dynamic and demanding industry.

84